W9-AXM-324

"I'M SORRY"

by Janet Riehecky
illustrated by Gwen Connelly

Created by
THE CHILD'S WORLD

Library of Congress Cataloging in Publication Data

Riehecky, Janet, 1953-
   I'm sorry / by Janet Riehecky ; illustrated by Gwen Connelly.
     p. cm. — (Manners matter)
   Summary: Describes various situations in which it is appropriate
to say, "I'm sorry."
   ISBN 0-89565-389-3
   1. Etiquette for children and youth.   [1. Etiquette.]
I. Connelly, Gwen, ill.   II. Title.   III. Series.
BJ1857.C5R48   1989
395'.122—dc19   88-16839
                                         CIP
                                         AC

2 3 4 5 6 7 8 9 10 11 12 R 97 96 95 94 93 92

"I'M SORRY"

E
RIE
235-1131

MANNERS MATTER all day through.
Say, "I'm sorry" or "I didn't mean to."

"Please" or "May I?" or "After you"
Will help you with what you want to do.

When you treat others with respect and care,
You'll find you have friends everywhere.

Say "I'm sorry" when you . . .

spill your milk . . .

accidently break your brother's
truck . . .

hurt someone's feelings . . .

leave your bicycle in the
driveway . . .

wake up your baby sister . . .

arrive late for the game . . .

forget to return your brother's
race cars . . .

let your dog get into your
neighbor's yard . . .

drip water on Mom's clean
floor . . .

interrupt your dad's
conversation . . .

say "I'm sorry" when you...

forget to pick up your toys . . .

knock someone down . . .

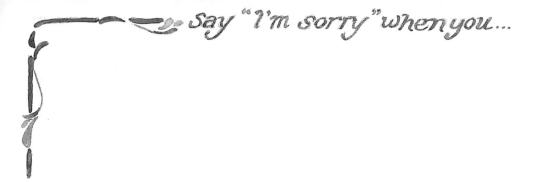
lose your temper.

Say "I'm sorry" to apologize
for doing something wrong.